Dan Coates
Popular Music Collection
For The Advanced Player

Project Manager: Carol Cuellar
Book Design: Ken Rehm

Dan Coates

One of today's foremost personalities in the field of printed music, Dan Coates has been providing teachers and professional musicians with quality piano material since 1975. Equally adept in arranging for beginners or accomplished musicians, his Big Note, Easy Piano and Professional Touch arrangements have made a significant contribution to the industry.

Born in Syracuse, New York, Dan began to play piano at age four. By the time he was 15, he'd won a New York State competition for music composers. After high school graduation, he toured the United States, Canada and Europe as an arranger and pianist with the world-famous group "Up With People."

Dan settled in Miami, Florida, where he studied piano with Ivan Davis at the University of Miami while playing professionally throughout southern Florida. To date, his performance credits include appearances on "Murphy Brown," "My Sister Sam" and at the Opening Ceremonies of the 1984 Summer Olympics in Los Angeles. Dan has also accompanied such artists as Dusty Springfield and Charlotte Rae.

In 1982, Dan began his association with Warner Bros. Publications - an association which has produced more than 400 Dan Coates books and sheets. Throughout the year he conducts piano workshops nationwide, during which he demonstrates his popular arrangements.

CONTENTS

FROM A DISTANCE

Lyrics and Music by
JULIE GOLD
Arranged by DAN COATES

From the Columbia Picture "THE GREATEST" - A Columbia/EMI Presentation

THE GREATEST LOVE OF ALL

By
LINDA CREED and
MICHAEL MASSER
Arranged by DAN COATES

The Greatest Love of All - 5 - 1

I CAN LOVE YOU LIKE THAT

Wods and Music by
STEVE DIAMOND, MARIBETH DERRY
and JENNIFER KIMBALL
Arranged by DAN COATES

Moderately slow ♩ = 88

I SWEAR

Words and Music by
GARY BAKER and FRANK MYERS
Arranged by DAN COATES

Moderately slow

I Swear - 4 - 2

I WILL ALWAYS LOVE YOU

Words and Music by
DOLLY PARTON
Arranged by DAN COATES

I Will Always Love You - 4 - 1

24

IN THIS LIFE

Words and Music by
MIKE REID and
ALLEN SHAMBLIN
Arranged by DAN COATES

From the United Artists Motion Picture "NEW YORK, NEW YORK"

THEME FROM NEW YORK, NEW YORK

Words by
FRED EBB

Music by
JOHN KANDER
Arranged by DAN COATES

Moderately, with rhythm

Theme from New York, New York - 5 - 1

34

OPEN ARMS

Words and Music by
STEVE PERRY and
JONATHAN CAIN
Arranged by DAN COATES

Open Arms - 3 - 1

From the Motion Picture "THE WIZARD OF OZ"

OVER THE RAINBOW

Lyric by
E. Y. HARBURG

Music by
HAROLD ARLEN
Arranged by DAN COATES

TEARS IN HEAVEN

Words and Music by
WILL JENNINGS and ERIC CLAPTON
Arranged by DAN COATES

From the Columbia Motion Picture "ICE CASTLES"

THEME FROM ICE CASTLES
(Through the Eyes of Love)

Lyrics by
CAROLE BAYER SAGER

Music by
MARVIN HAMLISCH
Arranged by DAN COATES

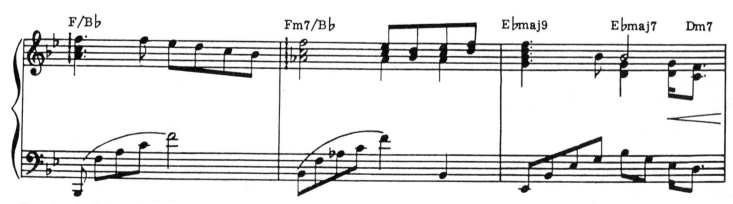

Theme from Ice Castles - 4 - 1

Theme from Ice Castles - 4 - 2

50

Theme from Ice Castles - 4 - 4

From the Twentieth Century-Fox Motion Picture "THE ROSE"

THE ROSE

Words and Music by
AMANDA McBROOM
Arranged by DAN COATES

The Rose - 3 - 1

intermediate/advanced

Titles in the PROFESSIONAL TOUCH SERIES provide the intermediate to advanced player with creative, melodic arrangements of some of the century's best-loved music.

BEST IN STANDARDS (Revised), BOOK 2
___ (PF0542)

All the Way • Lullaby of Birdland • Secret Love • Sweet Georgia Brown • Three Coins in the Fountain • As Time Goes By • Misty • What's New? • Night and Day • That's All.

BEST OF THE 70's & 80's
___ (PF0768)

Arthur's Theme (Best That You Can Do) • Brian's Song • Come in from the Rain • How Do You Keep the Music Playing? • Hymne • If • I'll Still Be Loving You • One Moment in Time • The Rose • Saving All My Love for You and more.

THE BEST IN CHRISTMAS MUSIC COMPLETE
___ (PF0735)

Includes: Christmas Auld Lang Syne • The Christmas Waltz • God Rest Ye Merry Gentlemen • (There's No Place Like) Home for the Holidays • I Heard the Bells on Christmas Day • It Came Upon a Midnight Clear • Let It Snow! Let It Snow! Let It Snow! • A Marshmallow World • Rockin' Around the Christmas Tree • Rudolph the Red-Nosed Reindeer and many more.

THE BEST IN POPS

Book 1
___ (PF0187)

Thirteen top hits including: Up Where We Belong • As Time Goes By • We've Got Tonight • How Do You Keep the Music Playing? • Chariots of Fire and many more.

Book 4
___ (PF0608)

Includes: Anne's Theme • Friends & Lovers (Both to Each Other) • Hymne • I'll Still Be Loving You • Kei's Song • Till I Loved You (Love Theme from *Goya*).

Book 5
___ (PF0756)

Alone in the World • Ashokan Farewell • The Colors of My Life • Get Here • The Gift of Love • (Everything I Do) I Do It for You • I Love to See You Smile • On My Way to You • Summer Me, Winter Me • When You Tell Me That You Love Me.

CLASSICAL CLASSICS FROM THE MOVIES
___ (PF0296)

Compiled and edited by Dan Coates. For the more advanced pianist! Includes: Romance from the *Piano Concerto in D Minor* (*Amadeus*) • Toccata and Fugue in D Minor (*The Phantom of the Opera*) • Pachelbel Canon in D (*Ordinary People*) and others.

ENCYCLOPEDIA OF SONGS FOR ALL OCCASIONS
___ (PF0861)

Contains 36 songs for engagements, weddings, anniversaries, sports activities, Christmas, birthdays and more! Songs include: All the Way • As Time Goes By • The Christmas Waltz • Happy Birthday to You • Misty • Night and Day • The Rose • Until It's Time for You to Go • Winter Wonderland and more.

(EVERYTHING I DO) I DO IT FOR YOU AND 13 GREAT MOVIE AND TV SONGS
___ (PF0726)

The Wind Beneath My Wings • Anywhere the Heart Goes (Meggie's Theme) • Theme from *Mahogany* (Do You Know Where You're Going To?) • I Love to See You Smile • Summer Me, Winter Me • Brian's Song • The Rose • Nadia's Theme • The Way We Were • Ashokan Farewell • Alone in the World • How Do You Keep the Music Playing? Also includes the title song.

FANTASTIC T.V. AND MOVIE SONGS (Revised Edition)
___ (PF0925)

Great television and movie music including: Anywhere the Heart Goes (Meggie's Theme) (from "The Thorn Birds") • Arthur's Theme (Best That You Can Do) (from *Arthur*) • Can You Read My Mind? (from *Superman*) • Friends & Lovers (Both to Each Other) (from "Days of Our Lives") • The Rose (from *The Rose*) • Up Where We Belong (from *An Officer and a Gentleman*).

GREAT POPULAR MUSIC OF THE 80's
___ (PF0621)

Contains: Always on My Mind • Can't Fight This Feeling • Hymne • I'll Still Be Loving You • Nothing's Gonna Change My Love for You • Once Before I Go • The Search Is Over • We Are the World • The Wind Beneath My Wings and more.

MY ALL-TIME FAVORITE MELODIES
___ (PF0824)

All the Way • Alone in the World • Ashokan Farewell • Brian's Song • Color the Children • The Homecoming • How Do You Keep the Music Playing? • If • In Finding You, I Found Love • Misty • Theme from *Nicholas and Alexandra* • The Rose • Time in a Bottle • We've Got Tonight • The Wind Beneath My Wings and more.

THE NEW DAN COATES ENCYCLOPEDIA (Revised)
___ (PF0562)

Includes: The Wind Beneath My Wings • Brian's Song • Chariots of Fire • Eye of the Tiger • Feelings • Love the World Away • The Rose • Stairway to Heaven • The Way We Were and much more.

THE ROSE & 49 TOP PROFESSIONAL TOUCH HITS
___ (PF0826)

Anne's Theme • As Time Goes By • Can You Read My Mind? • Cavatina • Evergreen • The Gift of Love • Hymne • I Just Can't Stop Loving You • Till I Loved You (Love Theme from *Goya*) • We Are the World • What's New and more.

THE WIND BENEATH MY WINGS AND 9 PIANO SOLOS

Book
___ (PF0698)
Cassette
___ (PF0699)
Book and Cassette
___ (PF0697)

Includes: Can You Read My Mind? (Love Theme from *Superman*) • How Do You Keep the Music Playing? • Hymne • Kei's Song • Miss Celie's Blues (Sister) • Missing (Theme from *Missing*) • Noelle's Theme (The Other Side of Midnight) • Once Before I Go • One Moment in Time and title song.